Primates: A Brief Introduction for Older Children

BRUCE M. ROWE

Editor

Christine L. Rowe

DEDICATION

This book is dedicated to my wife Christine L. Rowe, who has always encouraged me in everything that I do. And, it is dedicated to my sons, Aaron and Andrew, who I loved to tell stories to when they were children, and to my grandchildren, Ariela and Dalia, who are my new audience to tell both made up stories and things about the real world. Also, this is dedicated to my sister, Jana Scopatz, who is eleven years younger than I am. She was the first person to whom I told stories.

TABLE OF CONTENTS

Dedication iii

Table of Contents iv

Some General Information 1

Primates and Mammals 3

The Primates 5

Some Primate Characteristics 13

Additional Information for Parents and Teachers About Some Primates...........19

Glossary of Terms Used in This Book 22

Primates are Endangered Animals 24

Activites for Children...26

Websites About Primates and Related Topics..27

About the Author 29

Acknowledgements and Credits 30

SOME GENERAL INFORMATION

We all see a variety of animals in our everyday surroundings. We might see birds, dogs, cats, squirrels, insects, and a variety of other kinds of animals depending on where we live. We might also see many other kinds of animals when we go to the zoo, to an aquarium, to an animal park, or when we travel to different places.

There are nearly two million known and named living kinds of animals, but this is a small percentage of the number that are estimated to exist. Biologists, scientists who study living things, know of most of the larger animals that exist today, but many smaller animals such as insects are discovered each year. Animals can be microscopic or they can be very large, weighing tons.

This fairyfly (also called a fairy wasp) is a very small animal (insect) which is seen above under magnification. Some fairy flies are only .02 inches (.5mm long). However, there are animals that are even smaller. (Photo by S.E. Thorpe)

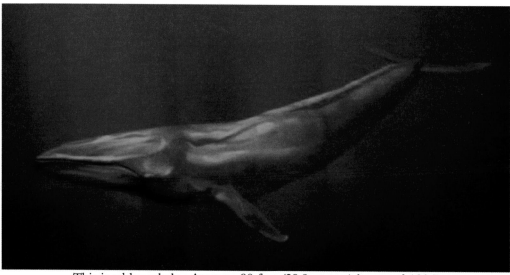

This is a blue whale. At up to 98 feet (29.9 meters) long and 190.7
tons (173 metric tons), it is the largest animal to have ever lived.

In addition to animals living today, there have been millions of animals that lived in the past, but that no longer exist. They are said to be extinct. An example of extinct animals would be the dinosaurs.

How do we know about living things that no longer exist? Different kinds of extinct animals and plants left behind different types of evidence of their lives. Extinct animals that had bones might be known from their skeletons and other traces that they left behind. Preserved skeletons or parts of skeletons of animals that once lived, or traces of those animals such as footprints, are called fossils.

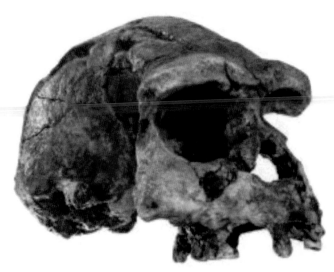

Fossil skull of an extinct ancestor to modern humans (scientific name: *Homo erectus*)

From fossil evidence, scientists can make educated guesses (called hypotheses) about the life-styles of animals, how they moved around, their diet, anatomical differences between males and females, aspects of their social behavior, and patterns of their growth and development. Unfortunately, many kinds of animals, plants, and other living organisms may not have left any evidence of their existence behind.

PRIMATES AND MAMMALS

This book is about a group of animals called primates. Humans are primates. Other primates are monkeys and apes as well as other lesser known kinds of primates. Primates are one example of a larger group of animals called mammals. In addition to primates; dogs, cats, horses, cows, lions, bears, whales, bats, mice, rabbits and many other animals are also mammals.

All mammals share a number of characteristics to various degrees. For instance, mammals are named after mammary glands. Mammary glands produce milk that is used by female mammals to nurse their young.

One of the other characteristics of most mammals, and also birds, is that they maintain a relatively constant body temperature regardless of the temperature around them. The body temperature of other animals can go up and down significantly depending on the temperature of their surroundings. Humans maintain a body temperature around 98.6 degrees Fahrenheit (37 degrees Celsius), rabbits about 101.3 degrees Fahrenheit (38.5 degrees Celsius), and a Blue Whale about 95.9 degrees Fahrenheit (35.5 degrees Celsius).

Mammals have hair or fur covering differing amounts of their skin. All mammals, even those that might appear hairless, such as pigs, elephants, and whales, have some hair. Whales, dolphins, and porpoises only have a small amount of hair for a short time when they are very young. Some mammals, such as the dog in the next picture and many primates have long hair covering most of their body.

A Long-haired Dog

Other mammals have short hair covering most of their body or a combination of long and short hair. And still other mammals have hair only when they are very young or have hair on only limited parts of their bodies as adults.

A Short-haired Cat

Many mammals have different shaped teeth called canines, incisors, premolars, and molars. Mammals with different shaped teeth might have different numbers of teeth and some mammals do not have all four types.

Different types of teeth have different functions. Some teeth tear and shred food and other teeth grind the food. Teeth, especially large canines can also be used as a weapon to threaten or attack other animals or to defend against an attack.

The teeth of some mammals, such as dolphins, and also many non-mammals, are all a similar shape. The picture of the skull of a dolphin shown below is an example of a mammal with teeth that are all the same general shape.

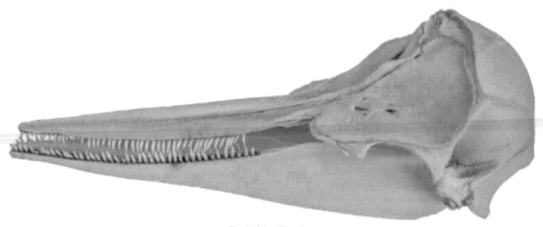

Dolphin Skull

Dolphins swallow their food whole and therefore do not need teeth of different shapes to process food before it is swallowed. Non-mammals, such as reptiles (for example lizards and snakes), and other animals which also swallow their food whole, have teeth that are mostly the same shape.

There are other characteristics of mammals that differentiate them from other animals. We will not go into them here, but they include a distinct structure of the inner ear and unique anatomy of the heart and the structures that deal with breathing.

THE PRIMATES

Humans have been fascinated by their non-human primate relatives for thousands of years and they have noticed the similarities in the anatomy and the behavior of humans and that of the other primates. These similarities have been studied formally, by early scholars, starting nearly two thousand years ago.

One example of a primate that most people are familiar with is the chimpanzee. Chimpanzees are very closely related to humans in many ways. It is not hard to see how their behavior mirrors human behavior. For instance, they are playful, they form close family and friendship ties, and they make a variety of facial expressions similar to humans.

Chimpanzees playing

By the way, chimpanzees are not monkeys even though you might hear them called monkeys in television programs and in many other settings. Chimpanzees are primates as are monkeys, and the two kinds of animals are closely related. But chimpanzees are considered to be a different kind of primate than monkeys. Chimpanzees are apes.

One of the most obvious differences between monkeys and apes is that apes do not have tails. Almost all monkeys have a visible tail, but none of the apes do. In addition to chimpanzees, bonobos, gorillas, orangutans, and gibbons are apes.

A Chimpanzee

A Baby Bonobo

A Gorilla

An Orangutan

Gibbons are called small-bodied apes, they weigh much less than other apes. All of the other apes are referred to as great apes.

A Young (4 months old) Gibbon

All of the apes are mostly arboreal. That is, they spend much of their time in trees. They swing, eat, play, rest, and sleep in trees.

A young bonobo, an orangutan, and a gibbon swing on ropes.

In most ways, compared with other primates, chimpanzees, bonobos, gorillas, orangutans, and gibbons are the most similar to humans in their anatomy, behavior, and genetic makeup. In fact, most modern scientists that study primates, think of humans as a kind of ape.

Monkeys are the next closest relatives to humans after the apes. Monkeys are a very diverse group of animals in size, diet, social organization, the environments in which they live, and whether they are mostly active during the day or diurnal (which most monkeys are), or mostly active at night or nocturnal. Also, most monkeys are predominately arboreal, although some spend much of their time on the ground.

Monkeys are generally divided into two large groups, New World Monkeys and Old World Monkeys. Today, New World Monkeys live in South America, Central America, and Mexico. In the past, they also lived in North America. Some New World Monkeys have prehensile (able to grasp) tails, which they can use to pick up items or can use to hold on to tree branches as they feed and when they move through the trees.

Long-haired Spider Monkey from South America with a Long Prehensile Tail

Old World Monkeys live in Africa and Asia. There is one small group of about 230 monkeys called Barbary macaques that live in Europe. Barbary macaques live in Gibraltar, a territory south of Spain. People may have brought them there a long time ago from Algeria or Morocco. Old World Monkeys occupied much of Europe in the past.

Old World Monkeys are a diverse group of 138 species, the largest number of species of any of the primates. A species is a group of animals that when males and females mate, they can produce offspring. Those offspring could in turn produce their own offspring when they are adults.

A young Hamadryas Baboon, an Old World Monkey, spends much of its time on the ground.

In addition to monkeys and apes, other animals are classified as primates. Lemurs, lorises, and tarsiers are primates.

A Ring-tailed Lemur

A Slow Loris

A Tarsier

Scientists call apes (humans are included in the category called apes), and monkeys *anthropoids*. Lemurs, lorises, and tarsiers are called *prosimians*. Humans are a kind of primate and therefore they are also mammals and they are a part of the animal kingdom.

Primates		
Prosimians	Anthropoids	
Lemurs Lorises Tarsiers	Monkeys Apes Humans (a type of ape)	

Primates can be very different from one another. For instance, they can be very different in size. Madame Berthe's Mouse Lemur is the smallest living primate weighing slightly over an ounce or about 30 grams.

Madame Berth's Mouse Lemur

However, a male gorilla (an ape) living in the wild can weight more than 400 pounds (181 kg). An extinct ape named *Gigantopithecus* might have weighed 1200 pounds (544 kg).

SOME PRIMATE CHARACTERISTICS

Like other mammals, primates nurse their young. Human mothers nurse their young for various lengths of time depending on many factors, but rarely after three years old. Among primates, orangutans nurse their young for the longest amount of time; up to eight years or more.

A bonobo mother is nursing her baby.

Most primates spend hours picking through their hair, a behavior which is called grooming. Sometimes they groom other members of their group. Grooming removes dirt, twigs, leaves, dead skin, insects, and other materials that get caught in the hair. Grooming also is a way to show affection and serves other social functions.

One chimpanzee is grooming another chimpanzee.

When chimpanzees and many other primates open their mouths, they appear to have "fangs". Those "fangs" are canines. Most primates have bigger canine teeth than humans. Canines are one of four types of teeth that not only primates have but many other mammals also have.

This chimpanzee is probably threatening another chimp.

There are some characteristics that distinguish primates, to various degrees, from most other animals. For instance, many primates have larger brains compared to their body size than most other animals and even most other mammals. This is especially true for the brain areas that control complex mental processes.

Primates also have hands that can grasp objects such as branches and pick up small items. Most primates have nails on all of their fingers and toes instead of claws. Nails are flattened claws. Among animals, only primates have finger and toe nails

Primates have eyes that face forward which is a characteristic that they share with some other mammals as well as many non-mammals. Eyes that face forward make 3-D (three dimensional) or depth perception possible. The ability to sense depth allows an animal to see how close or far something is from it. This is important for many reasons. For non-human primates, one of the main reasons that depth perception is important is so that they can judge exactly where branches are when they are jumping or swinging from branch to branch in the trees. Misjudgments could lead to serious injuries or death.

Forward facing eyes of primates allow for depth perception.

Non-primates that have forward facing eyes use their depth perception mostly for a totally different reason. They use their depth perception to track and catch animals they will eat. Of course, humans and chimpanzees also do this when hunting.

Many animals have eyes on the sides of their head. A four-legged animal that eats mostly vegetable material usually has eyes on the sides of its head because when it has its head down eating—think of a deer grazing on grass--it can still see all around. This allows the deer to see predators approaching.

Deer Grazing with their Heads Down Eyes on the side of the head allow them to see to their sides.

Since most primates eat mostly vegetable material, you might think that they would also have eyes on the side of their heads. However, they need depth perception to move safely in the trees. Most primates, in the wild, live in trees. Most of them also sleep and feed in the trees.

Depth perception also allows humans, along with other characteristics such as big brains and grasping hands, to make and use tools, drive cars, and do almost all other activities that humans do in a more efficient way than if they did not have depth perception.

As indicated above, one major trait that humans and some other primates have and that most other animals do not, is the ability to manufacture tools. At one time it was thought that making tools was unique to one primate -- humans. Then it was discovered that chimpanzees also made tools. Knowledge of animals that make tools has increased recently.

Many animals *use* objects in their natural environments to help them accomplish something. Gorillas have been observed using sticks to test the depth of water that they want to cross. Capuchin monkeys have been observed to use stones to crack nuts in the wild. Animals, other than primates, such as birds and dolphins, have been observed using objects in the wild to help them get food and to do other tasks. Many animals use objects they find to help them to do some task; however, few animals have been shown to purposefully *make* tools.

Using a tool just involves coming across something (such as a stick) that will aid in accomplishing a task, such as getting food. *Making* a tool involves altering an object in some way to better accomplish a task. Humans, chimpanzees, and some other primates make tools. There is also evidence that some other animals make tools, including some birds. Humans make millions of tools; chimpanzees and other non-human animals make a very limited number of tools. Chimpanzees make very simple tools when compared to most human tools. Humans use and make tools to help them do virtually everything; chimpanzees and other animals use and make tools mostly for helping them to get food and to process food.

A chimpanzee using a stick that it altered to get insects to eat

Among the primates only humans and chimpanzees purposely hunt. Of course today, most humans do not hunt for their meals. They plant seeds to grow food; they raise animals for food; or they go to the market or a restaurant to get and/or to eat food. However, in the relatively distant past, all people obtained their food by gathering wild vegetation and hunting for wild animals. Some people still do that today.

Chimpanzees (and many human groups) get most of their food energy from plant material. Chimpanzees do occasionally eat meat. Not only do they eat meat, but their primary source of meat is monkeys. Chimpanzees also hunt in groups. As with humans, among chimpanzees, it is mostly males that hunt.

Many primates form long term bonds with each other. Chimpanzees would be a good example of that. Like humans, chimpanzee mothers care for their babies and maintain a long-term relationship with them. Chimpanzees sleep at night in nests that they make in trees by bending and intertwining branches. Babies sleep in their mother's arms until the next baby is born. Chimpanzee mothers are constantly grooming their babies and often the babies, as they get older, will groom their mothers.

Chimpanzee babies learn from their mother. For instance, they learn how to make tools. Chimpanzee offspring stay with their mothers until they are between five to seven years old and they might continue to have a close bond with their mother for many years past this. Human children stay with their mother and other family members much longer than that, but chimpanzees mature faster than humans. For example, a chimpanzee at five is already stronger than most adult humans. Chimpanzee males protect all of the babies that they are around.

Chimpanzees cannot talk like humans, but they very actively communicate with each other in many ways. For instance, chimpanzees communicate by making noises that are referred to as calls. Calls indicate a number of things such as danger or that food has been found. In addition to calls, chimpanzees express emotions with facial expressions, and they use gestures as well as physical contact to convey such things as aggression or affection. They also communicate through the sense of smell.

A chimpanzee is being hugged by its mother.

I hope that you have enjoyed learning about the primates. Primates are a highly variable group of animals that includes humans.

Primates and animals in general share many characteristics with humans. That is one of many reasons why we need to respect non-human animals' rights to exist, and why we as humans need to work to preserve and sustain the original habitats of wildlife.

ADDITIONAL INFORMATION FOR PARENTS AND TEACHERS ABOUT SOME PRIMATES

There are about 695 kinds of living primates. By kind, I mean species or subspecies. Each species is given a name with two parts. The species name of humans is *Homo sapiens*. The first part of the name is the genus name. A genus is a larger group of organisms than a species. A subspecies is a variant of a species, but whereas members of different species generally cannot produce offspring that are fertile, members of subspecies of the same species can produce babies that when they grow up can also produce offspring. Genus, species, and subspecies names are italicized. Below is some information on some of the primates mentioned in this book.

1. **Chimpanzees (genus *Pan*):** All chimpanzees are placed into a single species (*Pan troglodytes*). Chimpanzees, which are often called by the shorter name "chimps", are medium sized apes that live in Africa. Female adults weigh between 57 -110 pounds (26 - 50 kg) and male adults weigh between 90 - 115 pounds (35 - 70 kg). Chimpanzees live in ever-changing groups, where one chimp might spend time with one group of chimpanzees one day, and they may move to be with others the next day. They are one of only a few animals other than humans that make tools.

2. **Bonobos (genus *Pan*):** Bonobos (*Pan paniscus*) used to be called pygmy chimpanzees. Although they are very closely related to chimpanzees, they are now called by the name that people in the area that they live call them. Bonobos live in the forest areas of the left bank of the Congo River in Africa. Chimpanzees live in the areas off of the right bank of the Congo River. Chimpanzees have a diet of both vegetable material and meat. Bonobos are mostly vegetarian, although they do hunt occasionally for small mammals. In chimpanzee societies some males have a great deal of power. Bonobo societies tend to be more female centered and not based as much on powerful individuals. Adult male bonobos weigh on the average about 95 pounds (43 kilograms) and females weigh on the average about 82 pounds (37 kilograms).

3. **Gorillas (genus *Gorilla*):** There are two species of gorilla, *Gorilla gorilla* and *Gorilla beringei*. Gorillas live in Africa. Gorillas are the largest of the apes. Male adults are considerably larger than female adult gorillas. Male gorillas in the wild can weigh over 400 pounds (181 kilograms); females can weigh over 250 pounds (113 kilograms).

4. **Orangutans (genus *Pongo*):** There are three living species of orangutan. Today orangutans only live on the islands of Sumatra (*Pongo albelii* and *Pongo tapanulienus*) and Borneo (*Pongo pygmaeus*) in Indonesia. In the past they were distributed over a large part of Southeast Asia. Orangutans are smaller than gorillas, but they are larger than chimpanzees. Male adult orangutans weigh about 200 pounds (90 kilograms). The males are much larger than females who weigh about 110 pounds (50 kilograms).

5. **Gibbons:** There are 19 species of gibbons in several genera. Gibbons are small-bodied apes (also referred to as lesser-apes) that live in Southeast Asia. One type of gibbon is the siamang. Siamangs are larger than other gibbons and have a big throat pouch that is used to produce very load calls and songs.
   Gibbons have very long arms that they use to swing from branch to branch and from tree to tree in the forests in which they live. The 4-month-old Pileated Gibbon (*Hylobates pileatus*) shown in the picture on page 8 will weigh between 8.8-17.6 pounds (4-8 kilograms) as an adult and the hair on its face and belly will turn black. Male and female gibbons are similar in size. Gibbons can travel through the branches at speeds up to about 35 miles per hour (about 56 kilometers per hour).

6. **Long Haired Spider Monkey (*Ateles belzebuth*):** They are also called White-Bellied Spider monkeys. These are New World monkeys that live in Brazil, Venezuela, Peru, Ecuador, and Columbia. They live in groups that change composition often and vary in size. The group can have as many as 40 individuals, but sometime an individual will be solitary. They have prehensile tails that are used for movement and picking up things. They weigh between 10.8 to 22.9 pound (4.9 to 10.4 kilograms).

7. **Hamadryas baboon (*Papio hamadryas*):** These Old World Monkeys were considered sacred to ancient Egyptians. They live in the Horn of Africa and the southwestern tip of the Arabian Peninsula. They display a large degree of sexual dimorphism (differences in appearance and size between the sexes). Males can weigh up to 66 pounds (29.9 kilograms). The maximum weight of females is half of that at 33 pounds (15 kilograms). They form groups of different types and sizes, but large groups can include several hundred individuals. They forage for food on the ground and sleep in high places such cliffs and rocks.

8. **Ringtail lemur (*Lemur catta*):** Ringtail lemurs are one of about 50 species of lemurs. In turn, lemurs are only one of many kinds of prosimians. Prosimians are primates that have many of the features of primates that lived a long time ago. Today, wild lemurs

only live on the big island of Madagascar off the coast of Africa and nearby Comoro Islands. Ringtail lemurs eat mostly plants and insects and both males and females weigh between 6.5 and 8 pounds (2.9-3.6 kilograms).

9. **Madame Berthe's mouse lemur (*Microcebus berthae*):** This lemur, at slightly over an ounce (about 30 grams), is the smallest primate in world. Its average body length is about 3.6 inches (9.2 cm). Madame Berthe's mouse lemurs live in Madagascar.

10. **Tarsiers** Tarsiers are prosimians that are classified into three genera composed of a total of 18 species. Tarsiers are small prosimians weighing only about 4.5 ounces (130 grams). They live in Southeast Asia. They have the largest eyes compared to their body size of any mammal. They are nocturnal which means that they are active at night.

11. **Lorises** Lorises are small nocturnal prosimians that live in India, Sri Lanka, and areas of Southeast Asia. There are two genera of lorises classified into ten species. There are African relatives of the lorises called pottos and angwantibos.

GLOSSARY OF TERMS USED IN THIS BOOK

anatomy The structural makeup or an organism or the study of that structural makeup.

anthropoid A group of primates that includes the monkeys, apes, and humans.

ape A common name that includes the small-bodied apes (gibbons) and the great apes (the gorillas, chimpanzees, bonobos, orangutans, and humans).

arboreal Living in trees.

biologist A scientist who studies living organisms.

call In relationship to animal communication, a call is a usually relatively short vocal signals that can communicate a range of messages.

canine Relative to mammalian tooth anatomy, a pointed tooth that can be, relative to other types of teeth, quite long in some species.

cell The smallest unit that can perform all of the functions that define something as living (see organism below).

depth perception The ability to perceive the relative distances of objects in a world that appears in three dimensions (3D).

diurnal Active during daylight hours.

extinct A species or larger group of organisms is said to be extinct when it no longer has any living members.

fossil The remains or the traces of ancient organisms preserved in the ground.

genetic makeup The totality of the genes that influence the expression of an individual's biological characteristics.

genetics The study of how traits are passed on from one generation to another and the study of heredity and biological variation.

genus A group of closely related species.

grooming In reference to primates, the activity of going through the hair (fur) with the hands or teeth to remove foreign materials. Grooming is also done to show affection and has other social reasons.

hypothesis An informed supposition about how one factor (also called a variable) is related to another factor.

mammals A group of animals that are characterized by mammary glands, hair or fur at some point in their life, a relative constant body temperature, which allows the animal to maintain a relatively constant level of activity independent of the environmental temperature, different shaped teeth, and other features.

mammary glands Glands found only in mammalian females that produce milk which is used to nurse offspring.

New World monkeys   Monkeys that are found in what is referred to as the New World (the Americas).   Today New World monkeys are found in the tropical areas of South America, Central America, and Mexico. Some new world monkeys have prehensile tails.

nocturnal   Active at night.

Old World monkeys   Monkeys that are found in what is referred to as the Old World or the Eastern Hemisphere. Today they are found primarily in Africa and Asia, with one small group in Europe.

organism   A "life form", that displays all of the characteristics that define something as living.   These characteristics include the ability to reproduce, to grow and develop, and to pass genes on to offspring.   Living things are also responsive to their environments to various degrees.   They can metabolize and breathe.   They are made up of at least one cell. They can maintain a steady state, but adapt to new environments.   Plants, animals, and single-celled life forms are organisms.

prehensile   The ability to grasp.

primates   A group of mammals that include humans, apes, monkeys, lemurs, lorises and tarsiers.

prosimians   A group of primates that include lemurs, lorises, and tarsiers.

species   The largest natural population whose members are able to reproduce among themselves but not with members of other species. Their offspring would also be able to reproduce with members of their species. In scientific classification, each species is given two names. For humans that name is *Homo sapiens.* The first name is the genus name. *Homo sapiens* are the only living member of the genus *Homo.* However, there are several extinct members of the genus such as *Homo erectus. A Homo erectus skull is* pictured on page 2.

PRIMATES ARE ENDANGERED ANIMALS

As of 2019, a majority of all known primate species are either endangered or vulnerable to extinction in the wild. For instance, all of the great apes are endangered, some critically endangered.

Habitat destruction is the major cause of the decline in primate and other animal species. Human overpopulation with the demands of the almost 8 billion humans for food, water, and space is causing what some people label as the Sixth Extinction, a mass extinction of animals and plants caused by human activity.

Primates live primarily in tropical forests and these forests are being converted into farmland and ranchland to feed growing human populations. Habitats are being destroyed not only so that they can produce food for humans, but also provide firewood for construction.

Deforestation on the island of Madagascar, off the east coast of Africa. Madagascar is the home to numerous kinds of lemurs, almost all of which are endangered.

The construction of hydroelectric plants and other structures, mining operations, and the construction of roads is also destroying the habitats of primates and other animals. Primates are also hunted for food, for their fur, for body parts thought by some cultures to have medicinal properties, and because they are thought of as pests to farmers and other humans who move into their habitats. There is also illegal capture of primates to be used as pets or for other purposes.

Although there have been major efforts to stop the Sixth Extinction, those efforts have been overwhelmed by population pressure and greed. In a section below that lists where additional information on primates can be found, there are some websites that deal with animal and plant endangerment and conservation efforts as well as the serious consequences to humans due to the destruction of habitats and the species within them.

ACTIVITES FOR CHILDREN

It is one thing to read a book or to watch a video on a topic. It is more instructive to personally observe the topics being discussed if possible. A visit to a zoo or a wild animal park can be fun and educational. The following websites suggest activities for kids at the zoo or after a trip to the zoo.

Many zoos list on their website activities for kids specific to their zoo. So, for instance the Los Angeles Zoo has this page: https://www.lazoo.org/education/family/

The San Diego Zoo has this page: https://kids.sandiegozoo.org/activities

You can check out the website for the zoo in your area to see what they offer for kids.

WEBSITES ABOUT PRIMATES AND RELATED TOPICS

Primate endangerment and conservation efforts
Red list https://www.iucnredlist.org/about/background-history
The Jane Goodall Institute for wildlife research and conservation
https://www.janegoodall.org
Primate Conservation, Inc.   http://www.primate.org/
The Dian Fossey Gorilla Fund International   https://gorillafund.org/
African Wildlife Foundation
https://www.awf.org/wildlife-conservation/mountain-gorilla
Chimpanzee Sanctuary and Wildlife Trust https://ngambaisland.org

Information on animals and other living things in general
The Encyclopedia of Life https://eol.org/
Catalogue of Life
https://www.catalogueoflife.org/portfolio/encyclopedia-life
Animal Diversity Web   https://animaldiversity.org/

Information on chimpanzees
The Jane Goodall Institute https://www.janegoodall.org/
National Geographic Kids
https://kids.nationalgeographic.com/animals/chimpanzee/#chimpanzee-with-baby.jpg
Chimpanzees (San Diego Zoo) https://animals.sandiegozoo.org/animals/chimpanzee
Chimpanzee (San Francisco Zoo)
http://www.sfzoo.org/animals/mammals/chimpanzee.htm
Enchanted Learning https://www.enchantedlearning.com/subjects/apes/chimp/

Information on gorillas
Gorillas (San Diego Zoo) http://www.sandiegozoo.org/animalbytes/t-gorilla.html
Mountain Gorillas http://www.cotf.edu/ete/modules/mgorilla/mgbiology.html
Enchanted Learning
https://www.enchantedlearning.com/subjects/apes/gorilla/index.shtml

Information on orangutans
Orangutans (San Diego Zoo) https://animals.sandiegozoo.org/animals/orangutan
Enchanted Learning
https://www.enchantedlearning.com/subjects/apes/orangutan/index.shtml

Information on bonobos
The Bonobo Page (W.H. Calvin) http://williamcalvin.com/teaching/bonobo.htm
Bonobos (San Diego Zoo) https://animals.sandiegozoo.org/animals/bonobo
Bonobo Conservation Initiative: What is a bonobo
https://www.bonobo.org/bonobos/what-is-a-bonobo/

Information on gibbons
Gibbon Conservation Center https://www.gibboncenter.org/
Five Fun Facts about Gibbons https://leakeyfoundation.org/five-fun-facts-about-gibbons/
Siamangs (San Diego Zoo: https://animals.sandiegozoo.org/animals/siamang

Information on apes in general
Apes https://www2.palomar.edu/anthro/primate/prim_7.htm
United Nations Great Ape Survival Project https://www.un-grasp.org/
Enchanted Learning https://www.enchantedlearning.com/subjects/apes/index.html

Information on primates in general
Primates: Apes, Monkeys, and You (University of California Berkeley):
https://ucmp.berkeley.edu/mammal/eutheria/primates.html
The Primates https://www.primates.com/welcome.htm

Information on monkeys in general
Monkeys https://www2.palomar.edu/anthro/primate/prim_4.htm
Monkeys (San Diego Zoo) https://animals.sandiegozoo.org/animals/monkey
Enchanted Learning: https://www.enchantedlearning.com/themes/monkeys.shtml

Information on prosimians
Lemur Conservation Foundation
https://www.lemurreserve.org/lemurs/ring-tailed-lemur-2/
Prosimians https://www.neprimateconservancy.org/prosimians.html

ABOUT THE AUTHOR

Bruce M. Rowe is an Emeritus Professor of Anthropology at Los Angeles Pierce College where he taught for 49 years. He has authored or coauthored numerous books for college students in the areas of physical anthropology, linguistics, and study skills.

ACKNOWLEDGEMENTS AND CREDITS

All photographs in this book are from Shutterstock except for the picture of the fairy fly which is by S.E. Thorpe. I would like to thank my wife Christine Rowe for all of her suggestions about the book and her encouragement to complete it as well as editing the final draft. Many thanks to my son Andrew Rowe for his comments and for helping me to self-publish the book. I would also like to thank my son Aaron, for making suggestions about how to get the word out about the book. In addition, I want to thank Iris Rowe for proof reading the book and making valuable comments. Many thanks to Philip L. Stein for making numerous suggestions about the book.

Made in the USA
Las Vegas, NV
15 March 2022

45694974R00021